The Sound a Raven Makes

SAWNIE MORRIS

MICHELLE HOLLAND

CATHERINE FERGUSON

The Sound a Raven Makes

Tres Chicas Books

Acknowledgements for each author appear at the end of her chapbook.

Tres Chicas Books thanks the Vessel Foundation for support of this project.

Book design by JB Bryan and Renée Gregorio

Cover & interior art by Catherine Ferguson:
details from the retablo *St. Francis & the Birds*, acrylic & ink on wood

ISBN :: 1-893003-10-8
ISBN :: 978-1-893003-10-1

Printed on 100% post-consumer waste recycled paper in accordance with
the Green Press Initiative. The mission of the Green Press Initiative is to work
with publishers, industry, and authors to create paper-use transformations
that will conserve natural resources and preserve endangered forests.

Printed in Canada

Tres Chicas Books
P.O. Box 417
El Rito, New Mexico 87530

CONTENTS

INTRODUCTION

We were sitting at dinner at Shoko's, Santa Fe's first Japanese restaurant. I never get saké because I'm always a little tipsy when I meet up with Renée Gregorio and Miriam Sagan, the other founders of Tres Chicas Books.

I was talking about the poets who have paid many dues and who I wish had more in print. The writing part of a life in poetry is bliss compared to the publishing part that often defeats us with its grunt and grind of endlessly sending out. I was saying I wanted to publish everybody whose work I love and started naming poets; quite spontaneously, Miriam chirped in, "Why not a book of the three of them?" It seemed a fitting undertaking for my next Tres Chicas Books project.

So, we have Sawnie Morris of Taos, Michelle Holland of Chimayó, and Catherine Ferguson of Galisteo, all three poets of rural northern New Mexico who share a deep language of landscape.

Sawnie is a poet I've loved for years. Her mesmerizing interface with the natural world of Taos has continuously moved me. Her work with *Amigos Bravos,* the wild river conservation and protection group, flows seamlessly with the liquidity of her voice, a feverish canyon of work.

Michelle Holland I knew from Las Cruces, where she was behind many scenes at Border Book Festival and Sin Fronteras. When she moved to Chimayó in 2003, I finally had a poet neighbor. We could ride to hear Saul Williams read at the Launch Pad, a smoky bar on Central in Albuquerque, or gossip about poetry on the phone. I was in awe of the work she did with Mind Graffiti, Española's teen Slam team, and I try to never miss their readings. I saw her give and give, heard her read, and love working together on the board of New Mexico Literary Arts.

Catherine Ferguson is my most devoted poetry student. I don't think it can be called *Teacher's Pet* when someone takes your classes for a dozen years, puts poetry on the front burner along with her prodigious painting life, and just gets so darn good by dint of effort. Catherine reads poetry deeply, meets with others to write and collaborate on book projects and readings. She is constant about her art. Her painting images grace this book, and the walls of my house.

It's time for pay back, and the currency is generosity. All three of these women have given to their communities, and so why shouldn't they have larger audience? This book took some patience and time, but each decent and necessary book is paginated bliss.

JoanLogghe
PROJECT EDITOR

MATAPOLVO RAIN

Sawnie Morris

for Brian

San Acacia

1.

We drove slowly toward the river —
siphoned down a channel, condemned
at San Acacia and under contract

between states — past the old church,
red and white warning,
gravel pit, aluminum trailer, and wary canine

until we reached the bed below — exposed
and mostly dry — like those stony
barren bins designed to cage what 's wild.

We leaned into the metal rail,
stood beneath the wooden sign,
pair of crosses freshly painted white.

Do not cross over the rail.
Do not attempt to fish or wade or swim.
Stay five hundred feet from the water.

2.

Always, I had to be in the water,
could not just look or graze with the tips
of my fingers. She, whom I loved —

afraid of blue, color of sadness — green
knowledge — tried to follow, to go
where I dove —

her eyes, her arms
like star points
flung —

3.

After delivering the first girl, gasping
to the muddy bank, he turned
back into the river, swam

its muttering surface, to search, guess —
was it here? or, there? — he'd last seen the other
girl's arms flail.

Like you, when he dove into
what he could not see through, the way
opened, as if a dam had broken, the current

released from inside. As with us, only the inevitable:
their bodies — the one he could not save,
as he could not save himself — cleaving

to the grill, not broken by the sieve, nor able to rise
amid mud, broken leafy branches, debris
and brown foam floating on the river's skin.

4.
She and he who died still dream
of her they left behind.
Three compelled to speak

without the help of shape
or matter. Between the gloaming
iridescent worlds: direct lines.

5.
We're miles downstream from San Acacia, now.
River-bed mud-caked, cracked by flash-flood,
drought, diversion, dam — still,

rain falls softly on this feral river
we imagine rising, sense its subtle dark
movement gather between banks

of polished black branches, alluvial
shoulders, its sinuous body lit by sudden heat
lightening, and susurrate in the evening air.

6.
To the west, the backlit mountain
holds its own green details:
our ride in a rough old jeep

open to damp air of twilight,
you, with borrowed hat catching rain,
the blue fleece that once belonged to someone else

wrapped about my shoulders,
the persistently undulate
river

How Strange to Wake

after long illness.

Your dog of eighteen years

out back in a grave

Next to a tree

not yet planted.

Under a blue moon

the drive north

Through Blood of Christ mountains,

Hauling the *other* body — *your own* body — in the back of a red Subaru.

A small door in the brain opens into color.
Surrounded by darkness — inside —

that's where we lived

All our lives

in that tiny Technicolor room

Inside the inside of the dreamer's head.

After Having Thought About It for a Long Time

In the warm springs where they
bathe and float together
her hand accidentally touches
his hand underwater.
His head jerks up in uncertainty

while her face remains nonchalant.
She draws back in a flutter
of sand, though on second thought
what she wants
is to take his hand

in hers, open
his palm to her mouth,
kiss the upturned flesh,
press palms together —
map to inner map, interlocutors

to separate pasts
locked in deaf-mute
languages of distress, frightened
by the sudden explicit gesture,
yet sprung open, exposed,

and imprinted with desire
to touch the beautiful strange forms
that grow from their upturned bodies,
innocent and supple as algae sprung from
alchemy of water, light, stone.

Shorthand in Leather Glove

I.

And what of those miniature gestures

                    meaning *sepulcher, fusion, colossus?*

Lines resembling my signature after fracture.
Name without identity.

                          Illegible scrawl

Reassembling the silhouette of mountains.

Elegant lineage (as in beauty), distinguishing mark (as in truth).
Unrepeatable river.

Recognizable shape among intimates.
Ashes, not really ashes

                  but bits of crumbled bone.

Sign at the beginning of passage.
Music.
The black box next to which we sputter:
The Lord is my shepherd, I shall not want.

Stones. Bones of the earth.

2.

The Taiwanese painter upstairs in his green room

      paints a painting of a rock. Rock after rock after rock

Appearing not outside (as in nature), not even in his mind (as in memory),

      but somewhere inside (tradition? practice? DNA?) his hand.

After rock, I would have learned pond, and after pond,

      lake, tree, and eventually bird.

Birds, the culmination

      unless I'd painted the human face

Of moon over river, water buffalo sloshing

      through rows of rice, next to the road

Where I peddled my bicycle

      past narrow-necked pots stacked thirty feet high

And stashed full of human bones. The intimacy

      of people and stones

In a single contemplative stroke —

3.

I will never be a Buddhist

    though meditation wakes us. How quiet

The room. Nights with only a candle. Turning

    my head in reverse, my feet

        at rest on the pillow

And pressed against headboard of mud wall

    soothed by my palms

And psalms of those I've loved.

Powdered orange dirt, brittle sage

    fleck and roll to the horizon.

Sangre de Cristos to the east, *Tres Piedras*

    to the west. Not that anyone knows

Who those rough initials belong to, eruptions

    in longhand, beginnings

To what we know.

ASPENS

I have nothing to say about this meadow, or these trees

Gathered in families

    of stationary dancers.

Ballet at the edge of conifer forest.

Nothing to say of smooth grace,

Or long-leafed fingers

    signing

In a furious fluency of shivers.

Nothing, nothing at all, in wind of applause.

   Moody. Rangy. August.

Mercurial silence follows.

Slightly swaying bodies,

    phloem of skin.

Alive, so easily wounded.

Graffiti of scars: human, ungulate

Visitation.

In this stand of a family of five.

Four of us

        huddle together.

The fifth singled out.

           Island

of gold, velum

           of green.

Rooted and reaching, underneath.

Language of branches, arabesque

Of limbs:

      one bends a knee,

One a gathering of ripples;

        strands of gray hair

Once curled brightly in spiral.

I think of the Pando groves,

Ancestral, spreading,

               and splay my arms wide;

When I am cold, they let loose

Their warmth around me.

Praise for this solitary stump

In the forage,

            the brown brush stroke

That brought into being its persistence.

Praise for the rocked⁄up and twigged,

Mosaiced

         and matted din

Of fern and worm.

Brilliant blue glare of day; blue⁄gray chill

Of evening

        descending.

Padded my feet. Knuckled my soul, my sleep.

I know nothing of aspens.

Among Those Who've Been Kissed

Plums and oversized apricots

                         in a red bowl

At first appear wooden.
The refrigerator comes to life.

Doors open

                  on either side of the house
Full of furniture and boxes, nests of the future and past.

Outside, a meadowlark sings with gusto.
Inside, love birds

                    cooing and exotic, country western and hip.

The rocker comes to a standstill.
The armchair, at home with itself, is draped

                  in a handmade blanket

Like a large man
Done with his day and ready for the television set.

The ache for it all is holier than you think.

Little Shifts, Here and There, a Fashion of Change

Now, the sound of a bulldozer

                                in the desert air,

A throb preceding reversal.

Now, the yellow shriek, a white semi

                      hauling a load of adobe

Up the midmorning breach

                of the hill.

The eye, like a wasp

        is caught

                in its mud-walled cell

                of requirements.

My feet are cold at night

                and grow flimsy at the foot of the bed,

                                  caliche and soil,

The diligent back-beat of weeds

                among arrhythmic flowers,

While the grass remains stiff

                in spite of this two-bit rain —

§

If I had this day, I'd draw blue strokes across it

with a watercolor brush

And live between each of the lines

— "dramatic

and wholly convincing" —

with a sliver near the end for translation

And a wide stretch in the middle

to lie on the unmade bed

and read or listen to the rat⁄ta⁄tat storm

as it moves

from window to window.

But I am a drunk

wandering between two lanes

of slow moving traffic

In a small town in the late fall just after dark.

Blotches of water

slide down the pane

With such stopping and starting

such jerky irregular music

The skin of the piano

beads —

§

It's difficult to live in a town full of tourists, in the suffocating eye
Of a storm

                at the center of a vigil in the desert

                                close to the ceiling, in this heat

Where the "hourly wage"

                and a "living wage"

        do not correspond —

                        like letters

Between two young words

        brave, but already broken —

Or a bridge from which

        the *other* was thrown.

Or where flight, by way of something remarkably human,
Is tired

        discarded and attempted in snatches —

On a good day I listen to a recording belonging to no one

        and dream

            of the previous color of my hair.

I'm an hour late, the traffic has died,

                and a few birds, here and there, are rejoicing.

It's also Tuesday. My mother is alone

with her new yellow dog,

while I work

in a lime-colored room off the plaza,

Homesick, and tapping the keyboard with two fingers,

in a manner not at all unlike

This *matapolvo*,

this day-after-day

Merely killing-the-dust rain.

Fallen Moon in the House of Speech

A solitary raven, black against blue,

rim to rim,

      early that morning she imagined
           herself being beaten — well, not beaten,
      but slapped around — a little — as a prelude

to sex.

The bride descending etc.,

        stripped down,
           broken, the desire to be taken
      apart — again — to be separated, that's all
         into something
    a little less solid, yes.
Spread like a fan (the one his mother's sister
      gave to him to give to her), or run of cards —
        the deck of a ship
    loaded
      and bearing down:

Oh moon, small small moon
Adrift, a' tilt on my watery floor
An unseen light shoots down on you
Looking up like a face, a flat pearl.

There's a gun in my mouth
And you are the target —

She can hear them — the disenfranchised, the locals —
        someone's uncle, and father, and cousin — above, on the rim
                of the Río Grande gorge she's heading down into —
                        her eyes on the edges — compulsive,
Perhaps, neurotic — repeated glance up — on the watch,
        the slow or fast hand,
                for who or whatever
        amid smattering of juniper and pine, stubby bush, cracked
                lines, a silhouette or shadow,
        the stunt man peering over,
                (as though this were a "Western") —
In a nearby ravine
                they're shooting appliances
      — *whine* and *retort* — *whine* and *retort* —
Ahead of the game, they practice.
The dead Frigidaire and rusting Westinghouse
        are brought to their knees
                among bottles, broken
      in the hard glint
        of sublimated revenge,
While the eight-hundred foot drop
        from mesa to river
              is blurred by dust
      and a subtle shudder
              in the late-in-the-a.m. yellow.

2.

The mind requiring a hand,

                yet gentle with damage —

      the tip of a finger, a dart full of ink

        or something

                on its way in a hurry

(Her sunglasses rest on the desktop at home,

              her keys are splayed —

                  perhaps tired

      of a ringed existence — as the clock

          whose heart stopped

    sometime in the eighties

            is digitally red).

What of that?

The hair on her arms stands

      a wheat-field from Texas.

The roar from behind — a bullet-shaped

      shadow with wings — dropped so swiftly

          into the crevice — in its glide, a sound

    violent with absence of living, no pausing or parsing

            not even a tilt or a tip of its brim — metallic

    and stiff with indifferent skill, the un-feathered wing —

          not just a plane — but a B52.

Does it help — as they say — *to give it a name?*

Though, *Just Practicing, Just Practicing*

          maneuvers for the sake of the "They" and the "Us"

    that keep being altered

         amid colorful television titles

              for each turn
                        of millennium war.
Who ARE those guys?

3.
Between walls of the gorge
          rocks might begin moving.
Above.   Below.   A detour —
          here
                              and
                  there —
          around boulders
                              already
                              fallen,
          sometime   thank god
                    when no one was around.
At night or late afternoon
              everyone — well — even the homeless are working
                        sides of the street, while out here in silence
                    (except for the wrens, the migrating blues & midmorning reds)
                        giants
                              have thrown
              these stones down — ENORMOUS — the size of VWs —
                    in annoyance or play
                                        or RELIEF.
Meanwhile, the river — the roar of its white hair
              and leaves spilling over

stones at the lower most reach,
not-so-still waters, not-so-green-
or-so-silent murmuring

the shoreline.
Do the dead grow gray hair deep in their caverns?
Or is that a metaphor (can we really say *just?*)
for consciousness — spreading out — a little
decomposition, or thawing, a coming
apart

4.
It's the stones that are cracking,
the bride amid all those dark lines
descending again the staircase,
her fractures blurry with motion,
her hard-bound copy of Janson's
19th and 20th Century Art, an ancient edition.
Spine a little off, a little broken at angles,
hair falling out
as straw from the red cloth cover.
Inside these pages, a solitary — or nearly so —
femme (Louise Bourgeois)
now living on chocolate
on the Lower West Side
where phallic shapes rise
like sponge from the porous
stone of a museum enclosure,

cells of old farmhouses
full of the instruments of ailing,
      (as though this *were* an old "Western")
even though
      the maker is French and terrified
of TOO MUCH SPACE.

5.

Continues, our walker.
      The road busting up
            in terms of vehicular traffic,
      reclaiming its natural
            rutted from run⁄off curving
      between cliff sides closer and closer to water,
            not the end, or at least
      never *not* the beginning.
            Blue where the light has not yet arrived
      or has already disappeared.

6.

Why that? — why her mother
                           calling —
frantically — it was
      to her, in her sleep?
Though on waking — what? — it was really — *oh damn*
      herself

raising her voice
    at her sister,
again, long distance, on the phone
       — hopeless! — the flimsy door
black metal latch
    doesn't catch, doesn't catch
but keeps on slamming (in the wind).

7.
The phone rings.
    One is tempted —
on a day such as this — not to speak.
    Even in the face of beauty.
Whose face is that? The mask
    becomes frail, collapsing in on itself
At the corners, cold rushes inward
    to town, while dark heads disperse
on a wind‚scattering plaza.
She hides in the house — an old woman in a car — recalling
    the bumper‚sticker: *Keep Your Laws Off My Body,*
    the first woman she ever loved *that* way,
the red Fiat forever breaking down.

8.

She'd like to write of the way back up,
        round of the corner, and lover
                whose figure is instantly
      identifiable, strolling eagerly into the gorge
             to meet. An *Orpheus and Eurydice* moment.
She *is* returning — maybe not all the way — at least
           she'll never be the same —

9.

Recalling the bed
        she kept falling into — attempting to rise —
             while the unseen
                   dropped roses
      over the rim. Roses kept hitting —
          landing — no,
Hitting her face,

As snow
        from an early spring sky — light
           falling onto her
                eyelids — that could not stay open
     — tried and tried — could not —
Following, now, the river —
              her fate —
       as in *obligation*
    willfully chosen — to enter —

Or shall we say

                it entered her as the music
Turns into singing

                           under the impulse
        to make notes.

POEM

Most mornings I woke slightly out of breath.
           Winded from the ghosted run
between the land of living and country of my death.
           I'd drag my dreams behind me
from bed to desk, write poems of sleep and ink and newsprint.

Ah sleep. Sleep and summer smoke.

From its cage, the fan purred a noisy exhale.
The mocking bird outside my bedroom window
           sang in all the local tongues and dialects.
Your car, leaving up the graveled drive,
           made for a lonely sound
                      and a relief.

The dog would rest his head on cagey front paws,
           make an effort at patience. The appliances would be truly patient,
              though full of curiosity
                  about what might come next.
The doorbell might have rung,
                if we'd had one.

I'd listen to the forecast. Sony by the bed and bath.
Bose above the compact discs and art books.

Radio news unleashed and born again.
Thank god, we'd say, for the on and off switch.

Then one night a voice from dream announced,
In one or two weeks there'll be a catastrophe.

Winds were driven.   Waters rose.   Levees broke.

What will you take with you? the dream
                    asked. Myself,
                              I said.

"ISOLATED ELEMENTS SWIMMING IN THE SAME DIRECTION
FOR THE PURPOSE OF UNDERSTANDING"
(from a postcard of the sculpture by Damien Hirst)

Dream I am swimming through forest
with room between each slender tree.
No air, no above or below. Gliding

through medium resistant
and buoyant as salty water.
Drowning never enters the picture,

though a lion
with big head of hair
has to be avoided.

When I think of this dream
of slipping among finely drawn trees,
I feel a longing for making.

Onyx tapers of swirled ink
seep into fiber of paper
lightly tinted green

and marked
by lines laid down
on open expanse once a forest.

Beyond forest, beyond writing,
longing for your presence.
Your keen mind.

To speak to that mind, also shaping
watery views from various rooms
we swam through. Windows wide,

sky, open mesa: rolling floor of ocean
dotted with sage: brittle seaweed,
jet black gnarly stems

and fronds of faded green.
You and I
streaming in and out of portals.

§

When I wake, my body is drenched
in sweat and the sheets between which I've slept
are patterned with stylized trees.

Among the branches of each,
one branch golden. The lion, I suppose.
As though the mind gathers the world

in which we're immersed, its smallest particulars
and in our sleep makes art. Makes us fish
swimming in the same direction.

Only in my dream, I'm no fish.
I'm long-limbed and slender, traversing with ease
an element familiar with understanding.

And you, wherever you are now —
isolated in one of many chambers
lined up and stacked in a city — you fin

through each frame, a multitude of frames,
with unified direction, while I remain
in the same house, in a different room

though between sheets and not alone
but in your presence. For who could have imagined
the postcard you sent last week, this dream

of ten years ago, and these blank green pages
with black pen would meet?
When two or three gather, a field is created.

In that field
even in your absence
you are here.

Your Last Left Note at the Start of Departure

And lonely is so much easier to bear when we are alone
The piano whose keys have gone into hiding
With not much in the way of an other and sometimes no one to love
Listen — on the other side of this curtain is power
Pulling up our hair — yours and mine both — by the roots
You keep busy moving your fingers — joint by joint — an exploration
Without getting past your Peter Pan collar
Your blue eyes trained on the everlasting ravine
I'm afraid you've forgotten to ever glance skyward — to look up
Like a telephone book with blank face and no numbers for dialing
Or a bank from which all money has flown
In some desperate and unfeeling corner your star was suspended
A relative dawn taking years to arrive
It's just barely enough to keep you from reaching
Into the coil of the burner — a poisonous snake bent on chasing itself
After all the speaking trees are a frenzy
Hair beneath our arms is a nest growing softer with age
Some days — I understand — not even the sound of our feeling
Not even the dream of a tail — your tale — can be heard
Ceasing to twitch in your cage — my hip hurts
From a future of too much rain
And my neck has grown longer the past couple of days
But let's not talk about illness — not now
Not ever — it's a terminal chamber in a room full of mirrors

The other side of clouds and under side of rain
Our light approximates the wattage of candles
You and I have a right to go walking like anybody else
Along the too-warm path of our previous hurry-up making
Such a cost — such a nerve-wrecking cost
I admit I had some idea of leaving
By way of lifting like those over-rated balloons on a Sunday afternoon
Ah — but here comes the sun again anyway
With its glaring but affable stare
Burning lines of a still unwritten letter
Into the desert of too much and always the same old
Perennial misunderstanding — a flower box of winter fear
In spite of all this the shape of my face is returning
And for the sake of cerebral vacation or lunch break or even a film
I'll keep on with our inside picture — including low flights
And too many houses — the annunciation pouring into my body
Here in our once wild neighborhood — the animals
two by two — beginning to reappear.

THE WATERY SOUND A RAVEN MAKES

The soul picks and threads
on a day bright with cloudlessness,
wind, and a cottonwood

trailing its fingers in feathery currents
void of water or rain, though a sally of ravens
caresses the air. Obsidian wings

flapping their skirts. Round dance in blue,
sky-filled quadrille. Inversion. Ellipsis:
trapeze without wire, without net.

Euclidian tip of a hat. Birds
entranced by tutelary gossip.
Mail box. Billboard. Garbage bin.

Their cackle and caw is rain
in the mind of the desert.
Uneven chatter of droplets.

Gardens thirsty and shy.
Large black birds
of middle-morning, circle.

Rock. Fence. Dirt. Wind.
Anguish of drought. ⌉
Passion of rain. ⌋

NOTES:
I owe grateful debt to Charles Wright's "Three Poems for the New Year" which inspired "How Strange to Wake" and "Among Those Who've Been Kissed," and also to Muriel Rukeyser's "Poem" which inspired my own.

DEDICATIONS:
"Aspens" is for Larry Frank. "Isolated Elements Swimming In The Same Direction For The Purpose Of Understanding" is for Ellen Levy. "Your Last Left Note At The Start Of Departure" is for Kat Duff.

ACKNOWLEDGEMENTS:.
"Little Shifts, Here and There, A Fashion of Change" appeared in *Chokecherries*. Section 9 of "Fallen Moon In The House Of Speech" appeared in slightly different form in *thedrunkenboat.com*.

SPECIAL THANKS:
to Joan Harvey, Christine Hemp, and Connie Busch.

BIOGRAPHY

Sawnie Morris was born and raised in Austin, Texas. She has made Taos, New Mexico her home since 1983. Her writing has appeared in *The Kenyon Review*, *The Journal*, *The Women's Review of Books*, and other literary journals, and has also been winner of a Texas Pen Literary Award and the National ACLU Creative Non-Fiction Prize. She twice received a Merit Scholarship from Vermont College where she earned an MFA. She teaches literature and writing at the University of New Mexico in Taos, and is co-founder of Amigos Bravos, an eighteen-year-old non-profit river protection and social justice organization for the Río Grande watershed. She is married to artist and environmental activist Brian Shields.

PHOTOGRAPH BY BRIAN SHIELDS

EVENT HORIZON

Michelle Holland

The Crayons Will Melt in the Sun

As we leave for the pool,
we step over a little bird dead in a speckled egg
surrounded by black yolk and ants.

My kindergarten daughter is worried about her crayons.
I ask her, "How do you know the crayons will melt in the sun?"

"It's in my mind,
I have lots of things in my mind,
unicorns and you.
You are always there."

The yarrow and sage fade their yellow and purple in the sun.
We need grey for contrast.
The dark damp tiled dressing room
echoes anticipation. It's hot.
I divide the universe in half, across the map of her small body.

"Everything," she says, "is in my mind, always."

We took the crayons from the car,
brought them to the pool
where the hot white deck registers 110 degrees.
She tells me to move the crayons, again,

before they melt. How does she know?
Her freckles bright across the bridge of her nose,
pattern out like chaos theory to her ears —
stars and colors go swimming.

The yellow plastic radio plays summer rock and roll
under the lifeguard — "walk!"

How can her little feet walk across the heat?
Brilliant water the goal.
The heat prickles the hair on my arms,
the top of my head.
A quick breeze, she bends at the waist,
head first she folds herself into the water.
Her eyes come up open,
mouth surprised every time.

Her colors don't fade in the sun.
No one else, everyone else, moves away from her
like ballet, her dance is rhythmic to the quick beat of her heart.
I hold her towel, and remember when I could cradle
the back of her head in my palm.
Her taut soft scalp broke my heart.

She says, "It's too hot. I'm too cold. I'm tired. I'm hungry."

And I am responsible as if she were still
riding out her incubation within me.

Our bodies will always be one, without language,
yet our separation pushes her away so she can warn me
about melting crayons and walk
alone across the pool deck, jump into the deep end.
The day rounds in on itself as she takes to wing,
her small shoulders sharp and triumphant.

Rachmaninoff in the Rain

So easy to look forward,
sit still,
when our white Ford van is in motion.
The purpose to go forward,
the wheels turn,
the wipers flap with the rhythm
of Rachmaninoff —
outside Hurley heading toward Deming,
our bodies float.

Sloe-eyed, the antelope turn their heads
in unison as we pass,
to the flourish of notes
compelling us forward.
For a moment, they stop. But, we don't.
The wheels continue, our speed
determined by cruise control
and the empty road in the afternoon rain.

So many layers between us,
we are content to look ahead,
knowing for the next hour and a half
where the road leads,
we lapse into the expected rhythm.

My voice, his voice, the piano, the rain and wipers,
my quiet, his quiet, just a ride between
where we are going
and where we came from.

Cool lines!

Isn't every moment like that?
A point of stasis, a hung-to-dry note,
between the compelling momentum
of before and after.
But, we can't stay there. The note
drops into the next relentlessly,
always a reason to breathe, to change,
look forward with Rachmaninoff.

COUNTER BALANCE

I've lost the stars
to the streetlights and the years
between knowing and forgetting.
My daughter doesn't see the patterns yet,
but she loves when I take her hand, point her finger
trace the handle and the four stars
of the only constellation I remember.

In this space,
our backs against the warm bricks,
hip to hip, we read about a silly bat,
lost and found on a night like this,
most comfortable in the dark.

Our knees point up to balance the dipper,
tilt it down to pivot and spiral,
suck us into the dark matter.
The open black is for us to live in for now,
and it's where we belong,
upside down by our toes,
our fleshy wings make the blanket
we will sleep in.

PLAYING THE RAIN

We wake to rain and wonder
where the leaks will darken the dirt floor,
where the pots are resting from the last rain,
and if we heard our eleven-year old daughter
midnight wandering again.

We imagine the night cloud cover moving,
and the glints of rain if we were to look
as into a shower of small lights.
Rain hits the corrugated tin above us,
fills the grooves into soffits,
into downspouts, into cattle tanks.

The corners of the tin don't connect,
they overlap uneasily, reflect
the light of most of our sunny days.
Water finds a way into our house
unexpectedly. The tar we slapped down
didn't hold, wasn't smeared
into the right corners, and we're leaking again.
"Oops," my husband says, his hand out,
"Get a pot."

We hear notes rise in the storm.
While we scurry for containers

to hold the outside of rain
that has turned to downpour,
our daughter is at her piano.

She matches the cadence
of drops on the tin roof,
the clucking of our wet hens,
the shuffling of horses as they find
a place to stand away from slanting rain.
She plays a song of this storm on this night.

Her fingers fly to the thunder
and her head bows low to the keys.
She brings the storm into our house,
catches the arroyos filling and washing
down small rocks. The echo
of lightning flashes with her fingers.
We place the pots. She continues,
and the midnight rain begins to subside.

She ends the storm as the only sound left
is the water dripping into the cattle tank.
As she passes us on her way back to bed,
I say, "Nice storm," and wonder briefly
if she had played the storm into being.

With Words Her Daughter Wishes

"I want to be a goddess," she said
without seeing the light generating
from her chest out,
out to her distant mother.

Mother, no goddess, inhales and spits,
shuffles dishes in the kitchen,
drapes layers of brown linen
on her glowing daughter.

What to do with a daughter
who cries for thousands drowned
in a monsoon worlds away.

What to do with a girl-child
too young to tackle algebra
who folds in on herself
when the bus is bombed in Takrit.

Her mother looks away.
"Snap out of it. Turn off the TV."
She hands her daughter sweet chocolates
and demands she eat every single pea
from her cold plate.

Hidden behind the smiling pictures
of an older sister, gawky cousins,
the good mother finds scraps of paper,
scrawled with words her daughter
wishes to live by.

"Don't take all the milk," she writes,
leave some for the morning,"
and the admonition her mother reads
like a prayer,
"Make the bad days go quickly,
live the good days slow."

HARBINGER

Autumn returns, claims
morning's bank of summer heat
gathered in falling

yellow poplar leaves.
Small, brittle lifeboats float
hazy twirls of ending.

Desert of rose dawn
outlines a gold-leaf sunrise
slowly disappears.

Blooms of summer gone,
marigolds and chamisa
herald the owl's flight.

A lone dragonfly
hovers, waiting over
monsoon's last dark pond.

Autumn's slant of sun
lies low on the horizon,
strikes the bell-clear change.

Chimayó Storm

one cool breeze wafts through
hint of rain, cutting heat waves
three dogs raise their heads

last rays catch red cliffs
cuchillo ridge gathers clouds
rain swallows us whole

Late Summer

Oh, green hummingbird
who thrums into my red skirt
I have no nectar

ARMS

Contemplate the heft
of automatic weapons.
Imagine the open mouth of power,
the words spilling our constitution,
our right to arm ourselves,
to speak our minds,
to raise our flags or burn them.

I used to pack some bread,
the white variety and a thermos of Kool-aid
and head for the cemetery
in late spring, when I was twelve,
when the tiny strawberries grew
behind the oldest headstones.
Under the drooping hemlock
I'd feed myself and share strawberry sandwiches
with the dead.

White sheets crisp on corners,
hospital bed upon hospital bed,
reflect the passive marble
we may rest under or pray beside.

The Temptations rang out our innocent decades,
when sex was free and peace
just a flower child away,
before the end of a hurtling century
whose tombstone will read illegible
the country we lost to politics,
to war, to genocide,
to mothers, their arms empty of children,
buried just under our feet.

I unfold my arms out
open my palms to gesture embrace
and it's an angry hope, not ignorance that rises
from my belly, round
like the river rocks that lie
at the bottom of the dry arroyo.

Our country gathers in the wings of a dark raven
that spreads itself broad over the valley,
where the shadow of war is ever present.
The moon rises over killing fields
here and everywhere:
Wounded Knee, Gettysburg, Cambodia, Mogadishu,
Iraq, Hiroshima, Normandy —
places where we thought we could overcome
the marble heft of death with bigger, better arms.

Want Ad

Bones and mud outline the victims
reduced to a grainy captioned picture
in the middle of the newspaper page "World News."
Round skulls pull back from their open eyes.
I cut cleanly around the want ad on the following page,
cutting up elbows and knees,
and large shoeless feet in the foreground.

I carry the ad with my resume
to the maybe job at the end of my drive.
Before I left, I noticed the apple trees in our yard,
and the kids yelling out back
swimming in the cattle tank we use for a pool.
Their image is bright and safe behind my eyes
as I drive the straight road
between Deming and Silver City,
flat with mountains far off to either side.

I squint to look for antelope
that sometimes leap in groups
through the monolithic cattle.
A coyote crosses the road
way ahead in front of my car.
A red-tailed hawk balances on a fence post
just past the copper smelter in Hurley.

I postcard the images to stack
against the picture of the dead I carry,
to protect me from the morning newspaper,
the nightly report.

But when I look ahead,
follow the asphalt, watch the wheels of trucks
roll close to the sides of my car, I whisper to the road,
"Who will trace the machete wounds
on the bodies of those people
who just yesterday watched their kids play?"

I picture my daughter's nine year old body,
hard, her neck always thinly layered with dust and sand.
I press my hands against the wheel, lean forward close to the window
and hum, remember my tight full skin, unbroken, quiet.

Event Horizon
San Isidro Parish Hall, Garfield, NM

"When you look into space,
you are looking back through time."

The wheels on the dirt and gravel
are the only sound as the cars arrive.
The sun blue February sky
is cool forever at the lip
of this place of divergent paths.

"An event horizon is the place at which matter teeters
out of the universe and into a black hole."

Four boys push out from the back seat
of the '87 Dodge Colt, and they all turn away
without speaking, like a determined flock,
taking off for the horizon.

"...while earth is our local address,
we have an entire universe to call home."

The two older boys each carry a .22
crooked familiar over their arms.
The younger ones range out from them

and back, pick up sticks and hurl each one
far, tilting their bodies against the sky and river.
Their backs tell us
they will shoot doves on the ditchbanks,
not notice the yellow stalks of before-
spring fields, the humped banks
where beyond is the sandy river,
not comment on its small grandness,
or whatever pulls the rest of us to gather —
write what must be written.

"Young stars often emit huge jets of primal gasses, including
a curious twisting pattern in a three trillion mile-long specimen."

The boys know their direction.
The pull may be toward great light
at the edge of their horizon —
a rise of mesquite and creosote.
Their walk, rambling out like newly formed
stars, and it matters not if there is talk or quiet,
away from San Isidro, patron saint of their fathers,
farmers, migrant workers.

I stay behind, a small pulsar blue and wanting,
inside the comfortable walls.
We will spell language,
try out words on one another
because we have lost their power

of quiet, of not noticing our own hands,
or the color of our faces
as we stare across the folding tables.
We don't want to shoot. We will not be lured
by outside horizons. Our explanations stop us from the edge.

"Not even light can escape its intense gravity;
the bright point at the center is the flare of heated matter."

I have turned toward a dark hole,
cold and echoing with the sounds
of our own voices. I must write
toward whatever small point of light
is left for me.
I am swallowed away from those boys,
their small hips, their darkness luminous
in white cotton t-shirts,
reflecting the yellow landscape.

"A black hole is 500 million times the mass of our sun."

But, in this poem,
I step away from the fall of gravity
I have always relied on;
release my small bird body
back to our mediocre sun
and follow an eleven year old with a .22.

(Quotations from William R. Newcott. "Time Exposures,"
National Geographic, Vol 191, No. 4, April 1997.)

New Dirt Under Cactus Branches

A story began after the fences were built,
after the Pueblo Revolt,
after the Spanish reconquered
the land where the acequias were dug
by captured Natives under the boots
of Oñate and his conquistadors.
In Chimayó, the story curves around the Rincon De Los Trujillo
where the remnants of sheep ranches
lean their weathered empty beams into cholla
and leave their rusty tin roofs to be swallowed
when the arroyos run.
A long story began when the old families, Vigil and Martinez
abandoned their wool for black tar,
left their sheep and weaving
to learn the profit of despair.

The wars, a world away, saw sons leave,
fields fallow. Drought took the high desert
and the connection of community
with water and earth twisted
to the track of a manufactured
and transitory heaven.
A family at a time turned their backs
on history, and found a new connection

with matches and a spoon
and an open vein.

Another chapter ended this summer
when the dirt road to the BLM fence
just off the rincon between abandoned sheep barns
became a noontime parking lot,
a hidden place to shoot up
for the teen-age girl
and her mustached boyfriend.
Their blue Honda Civic,
the windshield spider-webbed
across the driver's side,
parked on the flat brown dirt bordered
by steep hills of juniper, prickly pear and chamisa.

As the sun sets red against the barrancas
the raven pair that nest above the fence line
circle and swoop on a swell of air
over the tissues, aluminum foil,
abandoned syringes and Tecaté cans.
They watch the road becomes path a couple follows.
Against the dusky slant of light,
I see the girl from the Honda Civic
carries a cloth-wrapped bundle close.

They stoop, their backs curved to the ground,
the years on their young shoulders.

Their gestures are small and urging
as he drags a red-handled shovel,
they follow a coyote trail
and disappear into an arroyo.

Later I traced their path
and found a plush white unicorn,
a perimeter of votive candles and mica-flaked rocks.
A bouquet of plastic red roses
rested on top of prickly pear pads and cholla branches,
protection against coyote and stray dogs.
I leaned in to listen to the night sounds,
but no prayer arrived to mark the heavy summer darkness
or the small patch of new dirt.

Lifting the Image

"On an island of stone in the wind-tossed Sahara
a pair of monumental giraffes exalt the unknown artist
who carved them thousands of years ago."

I want to herd these giraffes,
the animals of my Sahara
who run down the hallway
trying to beat the late bell
knowing I won't close the door on them.

They "Hey, Miss...," and jostle,
hover above my head.
I have to look up, and I see them,
their faces open and awkward, expectant.
How can these boys be so tall,
so agile in their overgrown bodies
and so perfectly vulnerable?
What artist will carve their shapes in rock?

These students fall over book bags and big feet,
call out, and hope to create
some small wake for themselves,
like so many waves that will foam
and disappear into the sand.
Their youth will ebb,
the connection just a spare thread

"The silicone copy of the 7,000 year old
            monumental carved giraffes reveals exquisite details,
such as a line leading from the muzzle
of each giraffe to a tiny human figure."

I wonder that I am so small,
weaving a thin, strong thread,
a connection with the larger forces
and the timeless present that surrounds me.
My senior students, mostly athletes,
just don't fit in their desks, their feet out at odd angles,
squirming, sometimes bent over their work
so the desk is smothered by their shoulders.

We don't fit the room.
Can't we roam out?
Is there somewhere else we can go
follow a line to the Sahara,
lope with the giraffes as they have
for thousands of years without regard
for their history or intrinsic beauty?

What can we leave behind to gain
the glimpse of an existence
where we are the ones the artist reveres
enough to carve into rock?

(Quotes from Coulson, David. "Preserving Sahara's Prehistoric Art,"
            National Geographic, Vol. 196, No. 3. September 1999. 82-89.)

RELATIVITY

Einstein's greatest blunder was some stop-gap measure
to make relativity work —
something about anti-gravity and the space
between the stars. Something necessary
in the equation to prove stasis.

Prove the universe is a static net,
a colossal web wafting in some galactic breeze.
Galaxies, dark holes, super novas, pulsars caught.
He was wrong. And he was right.

Time and space bend beyond the edge of these lined pages,
beyond the toes curled into my brown shoe,
and my small speck of connective tissue
will be nothing more than matter
in a cosmic equation sooner
than the sun runs out of hydrogen, sooner
than the century runs out of years.

Out of chaos, atomic particles gather like minutes
to form morning tea and the quantum mechanics
of all I've ever created:
words on this page
words on other pages

volumes on paper, tossed, shredded, kept,
filed, published, and stacked into bookcases.

I've planted seeds to become salads,
or ideas to become kids
in a semi-circle writing poetry.

But, can I lift the fifth world from its moorings?
This tippy earth is sick of our footprints.
Underneath, the fourth world
watches our undoing, our unfolding
the nuclear fuels we will use
to exonerate ourselves from history.

Little stars, in our little galaxies,
we are surrounded by dark matter.
Our words will become our gravity,
to bend the universe, or to
follow the next one out of this world.

Trusting Pluto

I rely on that last little planet,
energetic in the cold, dark, out there
in its awkward orbit around our mediocre sun.
Pacing itself, passes as a planet, learned by school children
in the mnemonic word play of elementary science:
My Very Educated Mother Just Served Us Nine Pickles.

That one can leave, well, almost leave
the solar system and still belong
is the lesson of Pluto. So, I can waver
outside the rings of Saturn, past Uranus,
cold, in want of orbit or stability,
out of the family of planets, away
from any sense of gravity —
my commitment to mind over body
as tenuous as Pluto's to the sun —
and come back, know the warp
of my spin will return me to the family of planets,
mnemonics, the warmth of the sun.

Drink tea with me, Mr. Tombaugh,
and reclaim your discovery of Pluto.
When you were young, near the center
of science and life,

through peering curiosity and sheer luck
you noticed a tiny object, cold throwaway rock
on the icy periphery.

Clyde, I rely on my mind to make me well,
to turn me from nervous energy, backaches and fever,
to the person whose eyes see straight into yours.
Tell me about that planet, the ninth and last,
wobbling out too far one side of the universe,
and inside the orbit of Neptune on the come around.

You are old now, and the papers say
Pluto may not be a planet.
That eccentric pattern of pull and tear
may not be enough to ground an object to the sun
in any permanent arrangement.
Clyde, you need to pshaw this new notion
of belonging based on consistency and reliable orbits.

We are all out there,
spinning all over the place,
like colorful tin tops.
Let's talk some more, drink our tea,
than tell me I can leave,
and always come back.

Songs from High Shelves

Where the true notes rest
and endings are interchangeable
according to my understanding, or
the depth of my desire to understand:

How one bird in the hand,
or a wing on the rise of a clavicle
can lead so deftly to another.

Our connections remain
in our closed hands;
bird song rounded like sea glass,
amber and translucent green
in our palms.

One by one,
let's offer each finger out
from our palms until
the smooth colors take light
and send song out in a melody
we almost understand.

See, the only way to connect
is to let go, reach

for the top shelf, grasp
what is there like the gift
that it is,
our only chance to understand.

What's left is the weight
of something small in our hand.

SOLSTICE

The white winged bird rails.
against the bonehouse of the body,
aware suddenly of the limitations of spirit
in the scope of every day.

The earth rides our feet forward,
with a gravity we never chose.
Our hearts beat the rhythm that keeps us here,
in the interim space between before and after.

Now is all there is:
the table low and solid,
a curious red leather book that asks for opening,
other breath and paper,
indoor light, outdoor dark,
the comfort of wool and a fire.

I got dressed in the dark this morning,
unwilling to bring light into the house before the sun,
and ended up wearing trousers that should have been in the laundry,
and everything scurried forward a notch at a time.

I forgot myself again for awhile,
wrapped in the chores of life,

the comfort of the cage
where the white bird settles —
a giving up of sorts
or maybe just a form of patience
for the time I need to recognize,
I'm not the now of body and bone entirely.

Eternity arrives when I leave
the stones of my walkway
and the concentration of one foot
after another.

The Illusion of Progress

Guess the branches, the trunk
our lives trail out to twiglets
and we want to believe
we are the proof of progress,
evolutions greatest outcome.

All our synapses firing to Prokofiev
or Playboy. Our lives dependent
on the good will of society,
so civilized we fatten up the defenseless
and fry the guilty.

Give us a story,
the one that ignores variation,
the one that assumes essence.
We crave truth, or even the idea,
bold, beautiful, our perfect forms
reflected in magazines,
on top of cakes, smiling
at all the rest of our varied selves.

We are, we must admit,
the end of trend,
the only twig remaining

of many and many branches
that have long since vanished,
an outcome of inconsequential happenstance.

Remember, we are the ones
who insisted the earth conducted the spheres,
and the sun was merely our subordinate.

SMOKE

Early cold, colder than expected,
a smolder of kindling and paper
catch what little piñon is left
we mix with the old fence posts
we gathered yesterday.

The smoke wavers out
from under the Chinese hat
and we'll be warm 'til noon
when fire won't matter.

Smoke out this unrest,
there must be an answer
under the ashes, or in them, maybe.
Evenings are best to wonder.
Blankets warm, the day of errors
and almost dones over.
The smoke settles and we know
to address what comes next.

The calm approach will deter a fight.
The new combination of oats and timothy
will wean the horses off alfalfa
so they will enter the spring lightly.

The promise to not say yes
to another request,
no matter how worthy the cause.

See, this rising temper thing
that pits our tired souls against us
is a trial of smoke and surrender.

You know we're in trouble when
I climb into bed and don't bother
to move the dog that's between us.

Let's not wait 'til morning
for the smoke to clear.
I wave my hand over my face,
a gesture to lead myself,
and roll the dog over to the other side,
roll in closer to the warmth of your back.

Home and Hearth

There are spiders behind everything.
The toilet paper in the bathroom
rolls out a spindly daddy long legs.
Is he surprised to be beside me?
In the living room, from under the radio
I lift to dust, a fuzzy brown spider
scuttles down the banco.
One scurried from under the toaster,
and one rested nonchalantly
on your shoulder blade when you
took your jacket off.

It's been cold outside.
The snow that hasn't melted
is crunchy in the early morning, crystalline
and the icicles hang from the gutters
until late morning.

We are dusty here. Muddy.
Wet. The house merely an extension
of our outside world.
We keep the fires burning, so far
from smooth sheet-rocked walls
and the stick and stucco we left.

Snow and boots and mittens
frame these afternoons,
and I glance to see flames
from the window of our woodstove
to know it's warm in our house.

The dogs curl up where they can,
only anxious if we look up
from the newspaper,
look out toward the corral
as if we might leave for awhile.

Our lights are never quite bright enough;
the thick adobe walls soak up the wattage.
We live a dim world inside, brilliant out.
The horses wait for us.
What can't we imagine doing?

STORM COLLECTING

Our little blue Dodge Colt had no air-conditioning and the First National Bank registered 109 degrees on Main Street as we drove through Presidio, Texas. Six months married, still full of wonder at our unlikely, uneven affair, we carried like extra luggage our brash indifference to what your colleagues and my parents thought. I kept my feet up on the dashboard, my right foot flashing toes into the hot wind.

At four o'clock in the afternoon, and after fourteen hours on the road through three states, including the interminable state of Texas, the heat had not dissipated; the humidity was drowning both of us. We wanted to stop. After passing through Presidio, past the clock, we entered Pecos, Texas under a bell clear blue searing sky, and pulled into the first motel with a pool. We hadn't spoken for miles, just fought silently over the radio stations, working through the static.

In the middle of the late May week, we were the only ones poolside. In the west, the sun basked red as a blood orange. I stared and closed my eyes. For a few seconds the red image stayed behind my eyes like a brand. To the east, where the sun would presumably rise again tomorrow, great clouds had stacked themselves.

I'm from the east. I grew up with a small predictable sky. This billowing storm miles away loomed over the motel, over our poolside plastic chairs, over our new traveling life. I was far from home.

The storm, still far away, remained silent. The clouds dark on the underside rose through colored mounds of the sunset's rays, purple, red, orange into the brilliant white, curved against dusky blue.

The lightning broke from miles top to bottom, horizontal out to the sky and vertical from cloud to cloud. Far away, the thunder rumbled like conversation. We talked by the pool, swam intermittently, talked some more, our lives generating shared experiences, more about past than potential, and the storm built through the end of that day. The patio lights glowed like we were in an aquarium, and the humidity and temperature of the air matched the pool-green water.

The clouds buried the remaining glow of sunset. The lightning white and close, thunder following, pulled the rain finally over us. Huge, heavy drops stung as they fell on our damp, hot skin. I breathed in that storm, knew that we had joined its elemental force. Together we rose. You took my hand, and we went in for the night.

IGNITION

I am here to ignite.
Silence cannot exist without our ignorance.
Imagine each plate that moves beneath our feet,
as we slide imperceptibly
into mountains or chasms.

Imagine each step like Paul Bunyan,
the giant hero who dragged his axe behind him
to make lakes across a continent.

My chest fills with oxygen
that creates breath to fuel this fire
of connective story.

We don't know our power to enflame,
to engulf ourselves in the stuff
of Prometheus,
who was bound to rock for his sins.
He gave us fire,
and the flame burns from the inside,
a brightness behind our retinas.

I won't look in the mirror,
the vanity will reverse my image

and my eyes will flip numbers
like a digital alarm clock
tethered to the world
by time and deadlines.

The silence of deadlines and time
rests ever unignited,
criss-crossing the room I live in
like a technological spider web,
the lure of the dark widow in the corner.

I am hers. The hour glass of time
gleams red from her body,
the only fate I understand.

Take me back to Prometheus.
I'll run outside and look to the night sky.
I'll trace Orion's belt with my finger,
feel my chest rise against the momentum
of freedom only known untethered from time,
built from the fuel that will bring us to ashes,
then to connection.

I have timed myself
onto paper, yet I believe
my fingers can fly to the rhythm of words
kept in my frontal lobe,
read like a screen to form syntax from synapse,

to ignite the message,
the message,
if we could only reach so far
into the embers,
the message would burn
this paper to ashes.

ACKNOWLEDGMENTS

Harwood Review: "Relativity"; *Fishdrum*: "Trusting Pluto"; *Horsefly*: "Late Summer";
Journal of New Jersey Poets: "The Crayons Will Melt in the Sun"; *Lunarosity* (online
"http://www.zianet.com/lunarosity" www.zianet.com/lunarosity): "Arms," and
"Mixed Breed Story"; *Manzanita Quarterly*: "The Illusion of Progress," "Harbinger,"
and "Rachmaninoff in the Rain"; *New Works Review* (online http://www.new-
works.org www.new-works.org): "Counter Balance"; *Owen Wister Review*: "Want
Ad"; Shine On You Crazy Diamond: "Lifting the Image,"; *Sin Fronteras Journal*:
"Event Horizon"; *To Know the Dark*: "Solstice."

BIOGRAPHY

Michelle Holland lives in Chimayó, NM, with
her husband, 13 year-old daughter, two horses,
two dogs, a cat, some very fat koi, a few laying
hens and a nasty rooster, two widowed love-
birds, and four bunnies. She teaches English and
Creative Writing at McCurdy High School;
coaches the Española Valley's youth poetry slam
team, Mind Graffiti. For the past ten years, she
has been co-poetry editor for the Sin Fronteras
Journal. She coordinates the Poets-in-the-
Schools Program for the Santa Fe Public High
Schools under the auspices of New Mexico
Culturenet. Her first book of poems, *Love in the
Real World*, was published by Palanquin Press in 1999.

PHOTOGRAPH BY TOM HOLLAND

WHAT YOU MEANT ABOUT LIGHT

Catherine Ferguson

If you were alive I would give you the poem about you
in the plaza that year. February in Mexico, jacaranda flowers
falling all around, you squatted beside the ceramic jars smoking
a Delicado. I caught you with the cords from your hat tied loose

under your chin, your white shirt spotted with tree shadows.
We were sad, then we were happy, moving in and out of the
patterns of water from the well where the burros drank.

Waiting for the big trucks to quiet down, you sipped a beer,
I sketched you from behind your ear and then full face.
You talked to the man who owned the store, leaned against the post.
Two kingbirds sat side by side on a telephone line just over your head.

Like love birds. That's when I knew what you meant about light.
Because it was pouring down on us
from an upturned lake, washing the long walls,
the open gates and the horses. If I stepped

closer to you I would smell your hands. I didn't. Your hands
made of light held the brush that moved color across
the water.

You boarded the bus to Guadalajara.
It rained.

Heavy Equipment

I stopped going to my grandma's house
on Sundays.
I didn't miss the Gambel's quail in the vinca
or the agave's pointed thorns
in the driveway.

I just wanted to rub cheekbones and gnaw
on his chin.
I wanted to learn new things and stay in that mood
where you excavate a big chair in a dark room.

My grandma still went to church and wore the black mantilla.
I wasn't beside her to be hugged and introduced
after the money went around.
I wasn't there to watch the clouds rise
like dinosaurs above Camelback Mountain.

I didn't want to paint pink flowers with tendrils
on the black rocking chair.

I just wanted to play drive me and tow me.
I wanted,
            I just wanted
someone besides my grandma to wrench me down
under the grapefruit tree.

The first kiss he got was like one I'd give my grandma.
The next kiss was like a back hoe tearing up the earth.

Of course I ended up crying a lot
against the custard-colored fence.

Of course I wish I could have stayed a granddaughter
playing on the woven mat, pushing mesquite pods
into the mud wall of desert.

TOWEL ON HOT CEMENT

pooled wet from my dripping body,
coarse furred weave folded under my legs.
Burning hot where the towel is not.
Heat on my shoulders. Don't look at the sun.

I look anyway. The world explodes in white blindness:
I can't see Aunt Judy for a while afterwards,
and Grandma's body is as white as her plastic bathing cap.
Don't swim after lunch.

Time for a nap. The grape juice settles at the bottom
of my stomach. I dip my toe in the shallow end.
Must be time to bury something in the black granular
soil where the vinca begins. I bury my ear plugs.
I bury my barrette and my jacks and my Girl Scout badge.

Don't go out in the hot sun.
I walk to the canal while Grandma sleeps.
The back of my shirt sticks to my skin.
Always heading off toward a horizon.

Pick up a stick and drag it along the slats of a fence.
Sing loud. The dog gets a sticker in its paw.
Beyond the soles of my sandals my toes hit the ground.
On my legs a gray veil of dirt.

I think I'll go to hell because I put my finger in my nose.
I get so scared thinking about it. I think I have more problems
than anyone in the world. I worry that I don't have a neck.
Then I put my head in Aunt Judy's suitcase which smells like Coppertone

and Christmas. The first kiss I kissed was on his cheek,
then I felt like a fool. I wanted to bury something in the folds of his skin.
Bury my passport, my sapphire ring, my Little Women book.
After I touched him I thought I'd go to hell.

I never decided to drink or smoke or live with a man.
Come in out of the sun. Lay down beside me on the cool
cement. Grandma's bathing suit is blue.

Along the path to the swimming pool is a parade
of ants. A hand emerges out of the sky, pushes me along
the track of hours. I drop the devilled eggs in the dirt.
They fall and fall.

THROUGH ME HER LANDSCAPE

I knew she wanted me in the great swath of pale violet plain,
perhaps one lone farmhouse with a windmill,
or a corral. She would say to me: that's where I want to live!

Not the music that jangled her nerves, leave out
the way I painted shadows on faces. My grandmother
wanted to know if I were loving the land.

I loved it for her so much that it became mine.
Edited, my life was the cold water in the river that flowed
through Galisteo, was the blue sky in fall that tried to copy her eyes,

was a pink road that veered off in the middle of nowhere.
I wrote to her about the nighthawks swooping
over my head, a moon coming up behind the cottonwood trees.

Now I know I live here because I was conceived in a dust storm
and the seeds that became me fell from a plant that blooms
in the desert only one summer night a year.

I live here because the sky is bigger than the earth,
because my grandmother's body stretches out along the arroyos.
Because I wrote to her when she was alive, what joy I felt

coming home to red cliffs, turkey vultures circling the village,
a wall made of stone and mud like the wall around her house
from which I pulled straw
when I was a child.

MOTHER IN AUTUMN

Were you awake when I called you, or asleep?
Were you my mother, or a stranger whose face
caught my eye in the street?
Were your hands covered with oil paint,
or were mine?
How many times do I have to cross the river
to reach your house?

Did you tell me you didn't like artichokes,
or did I imagine that?
Did you turn down the covers on my bed at night?
Did you see me to bed and put your hand on my head.
Did you let me have a cat,
did you understand that I needed to know once
and for all about God?

Did you know how I didn't understand subdivisions
or high school?
What is a mother after you're grown?
Is it my turn to take care?
Shall I turn down your covers,
shall I fix you a bowl with grapes and three small
ginger snaps?

Shall I lay my hand on your head when you're asleep.
Will you let me drive you to some golden place in the fall
where we can paint, and where the grass is so green
it believes in God,
where the dog rolls on his back in the field, and the
water flows into its mother, and the purple asters buzz
like bees in the mist of spider webs,

the gauze of leaves twisting from their stalks and falling
into our paintings?
Will you be my mother in the winter when it snows?
Will you light the fire,
will you let water fall on your face and will you call it God?
Will you believe in the startling world?
Will I walk around with the word daughter attached

to my heart, or will I be a stranger?
Will the dirt road just flow right up the mountain
and will you let me drive while a smile begins to glow
across your face?
Will you bring the oil paints,
will your hand hold its bouquet of brushes,
will your hand know my hand is its daughter?

QUESTIONS

Were you waiting in your broad shouldered world for my hands?

Why couldn't I see around you, why wouldn't the cactus
let me alone why couldn't I lie naked in the vermilion
spines, I loved you desert?

Why couldn't I stand that boy?
Why did I hate dancing to "Hang Down Your Head Tom Dooley"
and the sweaty hands and the expensive smell of a white upholstered
church. Why did the boy smell like cologne and why was I so miserable
I wanted to jump all over Sarte and Buddhism?

Why was I born in that country?
Why was I born with a sword and a broom?
Why does my body fill with joy the way newspapers are filled
with print and thrown by boys across miles of grass?
Why when I leap does the road shrink to a spinning leaf?
Why is my mother small when I fly over her house?

Do you plan to stay in the forest? Do you want to lie on the beach, are
you made of shells? Is your mouth a drift of honey, are you a light in
the eyes of animals, do you wear your body under your clothes, do you
taste like salt, do you wait for me while I wash my feet in the river?

Have you buried your hands?

Have you burned my letters?
If I returned to your world would you greet me?
How have you arranged your mouth to say my name?
Does the cactus please you?
Does television answer the questions you ask?
What is the source of your flesh?

How have you chosen to remember?
Why have you painted over my paintings?
Is this the sunflower of you, or are you pacing like a bull in the vast rocks?

Was that other little boy in fourth grade with the dark hair named Terry Clark?
I imagined bringing him with us to San Francisco at Christmas.
Did he smell like my Mary Jane shoes? Did he smell like a new purse
inside? Did I imagine him in Aunt Judy's apartment combing his hair
with water from her oval sink, standing on the white octagonal tiles?
My hair still too wet when I put on my best dress, did I imagine he would
see the damp spot on my back?

Surprise

While he was at work, my mother and sister and I decided to
clean his house. Mice running between the torn bags of grain
on the kitchen counters, we mopped and sponged the tile,
wood, table top and sink. I swiped the bathroom mirror, drew
his red mustached face on the brown cardboard box

of his carefully folded laundry. We dried the plates, hung up the dishtowels,
stacked the scattered books of physics, mathematics, philosophy.
Swept coffee grains, beach sand, broken abalone shells into the
dust pan. Alone in the bedroom I pulled out a drawer to cradle
his socks, found black and white photos of Renee naked on his very bed,

her adult belly and soft breasts decorated with rose petals.
Looked down at my own breasts which were newly round. Quick,
close the drawer, his truck throwing off stones up the long driveway,
my mother putting away the broom. I stood on the threshold of his
open door waiting as he walked toward me. Thick vein in his forehead

pulsing in the late afternoon light, the bluest eyes in the world darkened.
Behind me my mother and sister giggled. In front of me a man
who has never seen my body naked.

Freshman Year

Suddenly I own the hallways, the dorm room with Lisa's perfume,
marijuana evenings in late September. My mother knows nothing
about Bob Dylan going around, Jim Brice teaching me a thing or

two on the couch in Paul's house. I feel adult sitting on the cold cement
step, stepping off the edge of the sidewalk by the pizza restaurant, I say
to myself: this is living on the edge. Jim Brice puts his hand on my bottom

as we walk up the hill. He's into drugs and I'm not. We sit is a small
green room. I find his face beautiful, like an angel. The green room
becomes a world. All the sex flowing up and down the stairs.

We go to a drive-in movie. The world is as small as the inside of the car,
windows all steamed up, and maybe I'm going a little insane with the
freedom, looking through Jim's eyes clouded as the possibilities of

reality. My mother comes to visit, stays in the hotel with the furniture
chained to the floor. She finds arrowheads in the dirt and suddenly
she is the child. I'm swinging over my childhood, entering a world

where I can begin to learn to paint. At night after curfew I work
on the painting of Leslie that gets worse and worse, smelling up
the dorm with turpentine. I can't get the nose right. Leslie spends

the time looking in the mirror pinching imaginary blemishes. Behind her the Janis Joplin poster, one nipple peering through long hair and beads.

CEREMONY: BURNING THE JOSS PAPERS WITH LISA

My friend wears a crisp Chinese purple blouse,
steps through the evening,
as ten years ago she stepped,
and twenty years before that.
I wear the dress from seven summers ago

                              Come and sit outside,

I say, trying to keep the dusk

        lighter than dark, but the trees deepen. Soon
        it will be morning, and she'll fly into
        the midwest and the future of this year.

        Three papers: the red with four green horses
running in a circle, the white with gold rectangle inside,
the two attached squares, one silver, one gold.

                              To the purple evening we say
what we want to burn: (wasn't my body safe,
was my body ever safe) the way we hurt ourselves goes
up in flames in the empty fireplace:

                              the dog comes immediately

to our cries as the old young bodies ascend the
            chimney. Some man out on a stroll
            along the river looks up, sees Lisa's twenty-years-ago-self
            that didn't know she was beautiful floating above the willows,

                        flash like a swallow against

the moon, and my ragbody soaring like an empty

            sweater, gathering speed, emptying its pockets
            of pencils and gardening tools, perhaps just
            some trick of the eye,   two *not-yous*
                              letting go their clothes

            their lies.

SATURDAY MORNING BLIND

If there was a bird in the locust tree,
                    I didn't see it.
If there was Bermuda grass crawling up to the
          front door, if the spines of cactus came on the wind
                    off the desert and scattered the yard
                    I didn't see.
If my father had not died.
If there was a horse across the street.

Waiting for my father to come back, as the horse
          returns from its rides, and the birds.
As the orange cat to the back door covered with wounds
          after being gone for two weeks.
No mother in the kitchen wearing a blue apron, Morning
                    divided herself into light, made the day
                    out of paper towels and string.

If there was a field of war in the dark
          I inherited from my father.
If the ground ran with horned lizards and Colorado
          river toads, I didn't see them.
If the trees were holding out their arms,
          I didn't look up.

His paintings all over the porch.
        His stillness, like being told about god.
The bathtub with the lights off,
        and the sound of thunder moving closer.

If at the horizon I saw a row of trees
and he walked through them, singing.

Morning turns from the stove with her hand on her hip.
        As if she understood him, and he just
                went out to check the hose.
I might have named the bird, the flower.
Instead I grew dumb, waited until I was grown
        to look at anything at all.

DESIRE

You made me want a tomato.
The tomato made me want a basil leaf
        and a room in the orchard.
I carried my want like a hummingbird
        and let it go under the pine tree.
My want flew around.

I wanted you, and then a pitcher of water.
The water made me want earth to lay my
        hands down.
A pear fell on the earth and I wanted to taste.
My hunger carried me around like a ladybug
        on your arm.

I drank from your light.

I thought I would stop wanting, but then I realized
        I wanted to stop wanting.

You made me want a slice of lemon.
The lemon made me want a pomegranate,
        and a view of the sea.
I carried my desire across the bridge to the water.
I wanted the river to be an ocean.

A star fell into the river.
A thousand jays flew up, all of them wanting me.
I had thought I wanted to be wanted.
The want carved my face with its name and asked
        me too many questions.

I said, I'd be happy just to trade this sky for the ocean.
I'm all out of desire.

You made me want rocks and shells.
Then I saw the rocks piled up by my house
and the necklace of shells around your neck.

Two Ravens

I said to myself let's go along the walls and the wind.
I said are you a woman or a man? When you do this
to me you are a woman and the wings end.

When you are a man you are dark and the tree
forgets its shadow when it sees you. I said to myself
let's fly over these antelope.

When you do this to me you are a man and
the sky holds me up. The roofs reflect your shoulders.
I said to myself let's follow the river.

Am I alone or are you teaching me
with your breath? Is the shine on your
wing grazing my tail feathers and when I turn

do your eyes swallow my heart?
Let's glide smoothly along this current
of wind, I'm upside down and the sun rains heat

on my belly and my back reflects the earth below.
I asked are you a bird or a woman? You are a bird
and your beak catches the water in my hair.

You are a woman and the sound of your cry
makes me hungry. You are a man and I am lonely.
You are a raven and I am the sky.

EAGLE ROUNDING OUT THE MORNING

I woke up to the yellow
      bird inside the sea of September.
There were so many choices to make,
      but I am only one woman.
So I chose a paintbrush wrapped inside a towel of wind.
There were a lot of avalanches in the road,
      a canyon I could easily fall into,
        great eruptions of pain that cried for attention.
I walked around the ruts and ditches until
      I came to a great plain of silence.

The only one making noise was the spider
      spinning its quiet.
I dropped the pain from my hands and watched
      it fall into the canyon.
The neighbors looked out their doors without
      understanding.
I started pushing the wheelbarrow back and forth
      under their windows.

In the end I left the face of a pansy on each doormat
      and went back to my house alone.
The Virginia Creeper had so much to say it started
      circling my ankles.

The flagstones all wanted to be dug up and
      put to bed again.
There were so many choices.
I had a field of silence inside me.
But I am only one woman, and the day
      has a million eyes.

TO TAKE WHAT WE LOVE INSIDE

I was ready. So we lay down.
My eyelids closed on your eyes as we slept.
Slender body against mine.

I was hungry. The day took off its jacket.
I took off your shirt and never gave it back.
It was that flesh you wore to my birthday,

stay with me, which I grew into, whose mouth
was sweet, whose arms had shoveled a city,
whose legs outlived their owner.

Quiet by daylight, your songs hid in their dark folds.

A butterfly of a man who invented systems for
collaging flowers, a man who never forgot
how to land on each petal.

Because of how I remembered.
How you forgot what we did.
How you hurt and I wanted daily.

Ground craving water. You moved the hose.
The ground drank. Penstemons grew
in all the crevices.

You are dying. my memory still holds
your thin back.
Painful tender kisses.

Once, I was hungry.
So the day fed me your corner
of the light.

JEALOUS OF MYSELF

That Painted Redstart bathing, feathers fanning
water like soft blades akimbo, dust flying, light
flying. I stood in the grove of pines.
Bill was alive, the Redstart like a bouquet of butterflies,
like a whirly hubbub of wings.

I'm jealous of myself standing in a meadow of iris.
It was summer and Bill knew where to find them.

The lagoon at night, water lapping when Miguel
shone the light at the Potoo. Quiet swamp guardian.
Me sleepless holding Bill's hand. Alligators moving
through the waves. The Potoo never moving.

I'm jealous of summer and the grove.
I'm going back to the dream, picking the flowers
to build a house. I turn the grove upside down
and shake out all the iris. House of blue petals,
green blades.

Pyrrhuloxia in the prickly pear,
deep blood-congealed-red.
I lay in the wash. Horned lizards ran through mesquite pods.

Jealous of myself living in that house made of iris,
running back and forth across the field bringing water
to the Redstart for its bath.
Shining my light for the Potoo and holding Bill's hand.
O this wonderful life. So jealous of myself naked
on the Pyrrhuloxia floor, feathers in my hair.

Too Bright to See

Just before dark she comes inside
sees summer, and him.
Making sure of the heat before she decides
to smile.
Making sure of the nighthawks buzzing the screen
before she places her hand.

Just before dark, and he's flat up against
the door. Making sure of her eyes, he squints
in the dusk. Trees brush the sides
of the porch. Making sure of the breeze,
and where it's poking its head.

Just before dark she's dividing an armload
of white daisies from goldenrod and fireweed.
He's in the next room lying in front of the
fan. Making sure of the time before she
checks the refrigerator for cold water.

In the dark she holds her hand, cold from
the glass, against her cheek. She hears the
enormous sound of his breath. Making sure
of her nakedness, she smiles. A white moth
flutters close to the open curtains.

Making sure of stars, then rain.

ONCE I LOVED YOU

before I was hungry. It came naturally, the fish
in your basin swimming peacefully were fish
I recognized.

You had forgotten your shoes. You were so light.
Swimming came easily then, and confusing your
body with mine

before I was empty. It came as a surprise, you
riding a horse I did not recognize. You offered
to carry me through the city.

But I was so heavy. Refusing you came naturally
then, and knowing your body from mine

before I was natural. Sewn into my dress by the way
light gathered around a mirror. Easily comfortable
in any chair, on the floor.

I could make love without a bed, as long as my skin
beheld an open window. As long as the dress let in
the light

before I was warm. It came to me naturally, wrapped
sea shell, sea horse, birds flying up out of the sea.
You had forgotten my name.

I had forgotten to swim. The fish walks on land,
searches for your body.

I Should Hate You

I examine hate.
Your ear on her heart.
Your ear straining after her words, and the gas
filling the tanks of my thighs as I step full weight
on the skate of your mouth.
I examine your ear.

I examine myself in the bath after you've left.
Walls painted red, my blood, my wine,
you drive off with my smell, the record shifts
on its socket after the song's ended but that
thrup thrup continues like the sound continuing
inside me that you made.

If I could live in the moment.
If I could hate.
Your ear on my belly.
If I were the only woman in the world.
If you wouldn't leave.
If I were not so gentle, not so silent.
If the marks I make on your flesh would last
through the night.
If I could examine your flesh.

If I weren't empty when you left.
If I didn't wake up with your indentation.
If your name weren't inscribed in the wall.
I examine the wall of my body.
I try out a longer walking stride outdoors
to the clothesline under the full moon.

I try out hate.
I try on the moon which you don't own.
If I were the moon would you love only me.
Lift the needle, set it on the beginning of the song,
the song that loves me.

I examine the song.
I examine my legs and my arms.
I dream of having your baby.

I feel the baby move in my blood while you drive
through the late evening desert with my smell.
What would happen if you saw me now wearing
the moon, cradling your baby.

So much mattered then, even the chairs you sat on,
your fingers in my mouth, now you're dead
and the hate lies on the ground like nobody's
old ghost.

Rough Night

Fallen apples in the orchard now much stepped-upon
pasty masses. At night baby coyotes yip and cry about the apples,
and ghosts of cats they kill hang in the tree branches.

Dogs across the road bark at the moon. I'm afraid to go to bed
for all the life out there in the yard, headlights of cars anointing
the tips of the spruce tree, lighting the wing of a lone bird

that insists upon staying awake through the dark.
I rake the overgrown grass in my sleep, but in the morning
apples still litter the ground, fermenting. And gopher snakes

move through them, stop like sticks when they see me watching.
At dawn I fear what to look at first. Oozing fruit, new firm peaches,

so fat and pink. What have the coyotes killed. Ground moving with snakes
and fat pink caterpillars that flip their ends continually. Datura
flowers holding their breath of white air. Hollyhocks struggling

above the weeds. I kneel on the earth as if I were praying to clear
the zinnias from coyote melon runners, smell so fetid. What mysterious
thing is my dog eating in the shade.

The bees stick to yellow flowers, no: white, but red and
     golden too.
I found them shooting out of the violet moon flower.
     I stick to
the deer's breast, seen from the window, and then I find it
     hard to
close back up again, harder still to find my way through
     thick weeds.
Trailing both my legs, I step over a snake in the middle
     of the path.
It's summer still, I pull grass out of bark and in this way
     the road
I'm on becomes a river, cutting through broken trees, I
     sense the
snake's hiding place, the many times I've had to shelter
     from some visitor's
prying lens. I cry out as if I were the one to be hunted or
     a child
hurt by the end of a warm afternoon. Poking a stick any-
     where the snake
might be, finding honey, and places where birds hide. But
     the snake
burrows in a hole that runs remarkably parallel to winter,
     rejecting

the greenness of August for privacy. I knew I would find
    a way
to stay in the garden. Something about the light folding
    back
on itself as I broke the day in half, laid my face on warm
    flagstone.
It will take running past the rakes and hoes, past the wild-
    flower garden
and the overgrown sunflowers. It will take finding wings
    but when I
look at you I don't want to fly. I come to the place where
    a shadow
lies along the late afternoon, and air is opaque. A sudden
    silence
catches me off guard so I scream.

Horse Out the Window

Dog hungry for morning, swallows cross-stitching the sky.
Horse takes up entirely the bedroom window.
Apples clothing the ground, ragged breathing shadow of mice.
Hipbones of a man with sun in his face,

                                    waves of light
hitting his hair. Wolf in me gnaws on only that night with the
meat of my body. Winter is coming. Apples become one with
the mud and snow. Windfall of pears reminds me of summer.
A lake of bird reflection melts

                              thin grasses flattening under
the slow dance of floods. But I thought we were friends. Your
blue ground, it's you then undressing as quiet as a deer in the
orchard at dawn. memories held in the meat of my body,
swallows climb the orchard, remember

                              Tucson, the many
nights I could not sleep, how it was never dark enough to forget
how hot my mind was, how naked you were as we talked, how
I could not see you laugh, but I could feel your legs testing me.
The dog's skin pink beneath his fur.

                              You told me when to
close my eyes, it was like drinking blood, june bugs hitting the

window screen, river of heat, river of blood, the green scratching
of the green tree. Yellow lights in the lake drinking black liquid
night. Keep wanting to remember mist,

                          the view of the horse,
dog staring straight out at its belly, my thoughts on the mane as
I heard cloth tearing. Hipbones of a man in the garden testing
an apple. Great big mountains burning off dawn as the horse
grazes and your ghost appears.

                    Instruct me.

FOR OTHERS ENTANGLED IN THE FLESH

Would you give up your eyes for me?
Or would you write with black chalk
that you never really loved me?

Would you sleep on a bridge in the cold for me?
Would you let the box of money tumble overboard into the dark water?
Could you live without money for me?

Would you run on a beach, your penis leading the way?
Would you laugh with me?
Would you lie on the sidewalk and watch the dancers with me and

that very night would you dance with me like you never danced before.
Would you leave me a note written with black chalk saying
tomorrow, if you love me, you will say "three swans flew over?"

And if I love you I will say, *No, they were geese, the handkerchiefs of god.*
If you love me will you let me lead you blind through the dark city?
Will your hand follow my hard body when I run up the walls?

Would you eat raw fish with me?
Would you wear my black coat?
Would you let me carry you on my shoulders about the streets?

Would you let me comb your hair with my fingers and watch your body
when you clean it? Would you lie on the beach
and let me cover you with sand? Would you lie on the bridge and

let me cover your body with mine? Would I believe
that you never really loved me?
Would your body know mine if you were blind?

AFTER A NIGHT WHEN YOU COULDN'T SLEEP

After stepping from a watery grave.
After stepping into the full-stamened white blossom.
The air kept being outside.

You found yourself up in a tree, or becoming the very
rattle of a dead branch separating from its trunk.
The air kept being tree-like.

You found yourself attached to the wren shielding
the rock from its great catastrophic noon.
After a fall in the river.

After watching mud cloud the pure water,
after watching clouds of mud billow behind your heels
as they covered the brightly-colored rocks.

You found yourself riding the magpie's back
as it dove into pink tamarisk.
After a night when you would not sleep.

And the day wore its feather boa tail.
Something made the clouds come over, accenting
crabapples as they wore their lipstick.

Orange-red stars in the tree. The tree kept dipping
in the wind. After hearing the cicadas start up.
After drinking pear nectar.

After watching the men take the tin planks off the
slanted roof. You found yourself dipped in light,
in clay. Found yourself a night of sleep.

WE DO THIS EVERY YEAR

Autumn on the mountain. Glittering air winding
up the road to the ski basin. Far slender trunks of aspen
cluster like violin strings between the larger trees
along the road. Eyes filled with variations of gold,

with tattooed bark lit by the sun to the west.
Dog wants only to remain unseen while cars trundle
slowly by, park to scan the view. My mother and I
set up our paints beside the car, dab color and

mood. Nothing much to be said as deer hide,
as gray jays refuse to forgive the complex human traffic.
Chickadee sings, attention paid now to patchwork color,
rusts and ambers, deep green flowing down the mountains

like sheets of dark water. Soon we will also descend
with the trembling dog, our pictures swiped to the edge
viridian, cadmium yellow. I refuse to argue. Gold
so gold, sky so blue. Is there such a thing as real life,

where color does not turn? Real night closing on blaze.
I lie in bed, happy and alone, insisting on what the mountain
is carrying in its upturned mouth, even in the dark, I know
the deer have moved to the open, surrounding themselves

with the view of space that they reclaim. Night. Owls reflect
the nascent gold, shimmering. As my painting insists some
singing afternoon even from the wall.

You promised me two kingbirds if I could see them
      clinging
to the telephone line. I never looked back much.

My mother kept leaving. You don't have to tell me
      how often I mention my mother.

I think of you even though you've been dead for years.
In fact, here I am in the car talking to you while I wait
      to be educated.

You're with me more than ever. If I vibrate intensely
      enough in this holy 4:00 afternoon light will you
            materialize in the passenger seat with the sun
                  shining too hot on your pants?

Will someone alive ever take your place?

How I notice things, and then want to close my eyes,
      all the noticing we did, but me standing outside your door
           and down the hill. How long have I lived alone.

How long have I relied on no one.
      They ask me strange questions. "Have you been here long?"
      I hear the crow flying over your grave.

I miss my hand painting a picture even though it was
    yesterday. I miss my voice saying your name and my mouth
        filling with you.

You promised me two sunsets and one half moon
    if I could see it.

Two Bells

Two thrusts in the compost by the used-up tomato cages, two ghosts
worshipping the topsoil. I sit in her garden, untouched since
last year: purple tips of oat grass panicles sway between
hollyhocks and sow thistle. Moon and sun pass each other
in a brief pas-de-deux while Maria Christina pours olive oil
in the skillet and I fill the squares of the crossword.

Two glasses of wine on the counter, two plates receive tomato,
cilantro, goat cheese. I want to talk about death. We sit in a slit of
evening so lovely that I can hardly speak. Two robins rattle the willow
branches against the fence, two hands pull apart flat ciabatta.

What if when we die we'll be sitting here, feeling ghosts tunneling
in the heaven and hell beneath the willow roots. And we will laugh
how we worried so much about what to eat and how to think,
when all that was going to happen was this eternally moving into the night,
dog smelling his paw in the dappled shade, a raspberry cane
growing up through the gray rotten wood of the deck.

Two black swaths of sky wash across the moon, two women in love
with the kitchen light after dark. Washing plates, matching the sizes
of spoons. Their bodies as precious and porous as time, which
advances inside them, illuminating their wet hands.

SHADOWS

I have walked here before. but
never in this darkness smothered with light,
this day carrying its load of night.

My loneliness stampedes the fences.

In a pasture, sweet mustard higher than my knees.
I see curtains in the windows of an old adobe next to the field.

Voices of mud in the bosque, puddles sucking me down.

                                              Spring again.
I hold on to the earth so hard it begins to sway beneath me.
I could not live without the shadows of cottonwood trees crossing the

road,
without the doves answering themselves.

Tonight: full moon. Time to plant seeds in the face
of no arm encircling my waist.

I WANT

If the hillside cracked and showed me its bones.
If the ripped sky revealed its corsets and undershirts.

Cactus to live inside me, shade to be South Tucson's
Mexican restaurants I creep into at noon
out of the concrete sun.

> I can be a terrifying skull of a daughter who poisons
> the little spring in the forest.

> But don't let me fool you. If you have never had children
> you would understand. I want to be your child,

and the garage to sleep and let go of its car. To sleep without
the smell of the engine and the oil drip.

If I could swim salt and fish, I would want.

> I want to be your car.
I want you to show me the roads you took in Italy.
Shine a light on everything that hurts me.

Summer will save me with its wet blue chair.

ACKNOWLEDGMENTS
Cover and interior artwork are details from her retablo *St. Francis & the Birds,*
acrylic & ink on wood.

BIOGRAPHY

Catherine Ferguson is a poet and painter living in
Galisteo, New Mexico, where she gardens and
walks her dog. Since 1973, she has been painting
retablos, a New Mexico tradition. Inspired by
landscape, animals, and trees, she creates
watercolors, oils, and poems that express her love
for nature. Catherine teaches retablo and water-
color painting.

PHOTOGRAPH BY JUDY TUWALETSTIWA

Set in Poliphilus & Blado italic.
Poliphilus was part of Stanley Morison's revival program
at Monotype Corporation and released in 1923. It is based on
the *Hypernerotomachia Poliphili* printed by Aldus Manutius
in Venice in 1499. Irregularities from the original type impression
were retained and give it a rustic warmth. The italic is Blado
and it is based on the chancery style of Antonio Blado,
sixteenth-century calligrapher and printer who lived in Rome.

Kali is an aspect of the great goddess Devi, the most complex and powerful
of the goddesses. Kali is one of the fiercer aspects of Devi, but nonetheless as
Shiva's consort, she represents female energy. Kali's aspect is destructive
and all-pervading, as she represents the power or energy of time. Her
four arms represent the four directions of space identified with the complete
cycle of time. Kali is beyond time, beyond fear . . . her giving hand shows
she is the giver of bliss. Because she represents a stage beyond all
attachment, she appears fearful to us. So, she has a dual aspect—
both destroyer of all that exists and the giver of eternal peace.

This image is from drawings by women of Mithila, India.

OTHER TITLES BY TRES CHICAS BOOKS

Rice
Joan Logghe, 2004

Water Shed
Renée Gregorio, 2004

Just Outside the Frame: Poets from the Santa Fe Poetry Broadside,
edited by Miriam Bobkoff and Miriam Sagan, 2005

Big Thank You
JB Bryan, 2006

Water Shining Beyond the Fields
John Brandi, 2006

All Tres Chicas Book titles are available directly from the publishers at
reneeclaire@cybermesa.com
joanlogghe@hotmail.com
msagan1035@aol.com
or on the web at Amazon.com
& Small Press Distribution at spdbooks.org